Ken,

Be a great
leader for Him!

Chris Marshall

Lessons on
LEADERSHIP

Chet R. Marshall • Foreword by Zig Ziglar

ELEVATION EXPRESS PUBLISHING
Hurricane, WV

Elevation Express Publishing Company
130 Summit Ridge
Hurricane, WV 25526
Publisher's Cataloging-in-Publication Data
Marshall, Chet R.

Lessons on leadership : visualizing qualities of a leader / Chet R. Marshall -- Hurricane, WV : Elevation Express, 2003.

p ; cm.

ISBN 0-9726436-0-5

1. Leadership. 2. Management.

HD57.7 .M37 2003
658.4092—dc21   0302

Project coordination by Jenkins Group, Inc. • www.bookpublishing.com
Cover design by Kelli Leader
Interior design by Barb Hodge

Printed in China

07 06 05 04 03 * 5 4 3 2 1

Contents

About the Author

Chet Marshall is a rare find in the arena of professional speaking. His rich background in the corporate world includes several years in healthcare administration, finance, manufacturing, retail (as a franchisee and franchiser) and entrepreneurship as a general partner for a venture capital partnership. An experienced CEO in several industries, Chet is an expert on leadership and management, and has spoken on both topics for over 25 years. He is also the author of *Lessons Learned from Bosses on How to be a Boss*, *My World Peace Can Be Your World Peace* and co-author of *Wholehearted Success, Thriving in the Midst of Change* and *Magnetic Leadership*.

An avid world traveler, Chet's speaking career has taken him to all 50 states and most of Canada. He is a member of the National Speakers Association and also the 2002-2003 Chairman of the association's Motivational PEG (Professional Expert Group). Chet's focus is on elevation, "taking leaders and professionals to the next level" and overcoming life's challenges. His warm and refreshing sense of humor sparks all of his presentations and his characters are very popular. Chet is also active with the Fellowship of Christian Athletes and spends considerable time working with youth, encouraging their growth and success. His zeal for helping others earned him the AAA Meritorious Service Award. If you're looking for powerful, humorous and meaningful all wrapped up in one creative package, Chet is the right speaker for your event.

Contact Information:
Chet R. Marshall
Elevation Express
130 Summit Ridge
Hurricane, WV 25526
Tel: (304) 545-5100, Fax: (304) 757-5651
Email: chetinwv@aol.com
www.elevationexpress.com

Elevation Express—*"Taking Leaders to the Next Level"*
And
Elevation Learning Systems, LLC,
"Taking Professionals to the Next Level"
Using
The Og Manadino Success System
"Becoming the Greatest Healthcare Professional and the Greatest You"

Acknowledgements

I would like to thank my friend and mentor Dr. Sheila Murray Bethel for her encouragement to continue to "make a difference" as she has for so many years in the area of leadership. She has truly been a trusted friend in guiding me in my professional career.

Also, I would like to thank Zig Ziglar who has been a true inspiration to me as he has been to thousands of others. His life's challenges to get "to the top" gave me the drive to aspire to be a professional speaker and author.

I would also like to honor my mother for the years of what I call "Momma's philosophies" and for always believing in me. Without her spiritual guidance, my life would have been much different and I would not have realized the need to make a difference in other people's lives. Thank you, Mom. I love you.

Foreword by Zig Ziglar

Lessons on Leadership—Visualizing Qualities of a Leader is the classic demonstration of God's Word when it says, "a little child shall lead them." Chet Marshall has managed to capture the wisdom of a child from a biblical perspective and convert it into practical, everyday procedures we can use in our lives as they relate to our personal, family, and professional lives.

The principles are so clear and the messages so abundant that not only can a small child depict them, an adult can profit from them. In a few short pages and in an entertaining manner, Chet Marshall has directed us toward the qualities that separate leaders from followers. And yet in no way is this offensive to those who follow. In the process of identifying leadership qualities, followers learn lessons that, when applied, will convert them to leaders. No stone is left unturned, and yet no one can be confused about what makes a leader and how leaders make a difference. Just as genuine leaders do whatever it takes, *Lessons on Leadership—Visualizing Qualities of a Leader* gives those leaders and would-be leaders clear, specific directions on successful leadership. Good stuff.

Zig Ziglar
Author/Motivational Teacher

Introduction

Leadership and Kayla
"...and a little child shall lead them"

"*Chester is a leader in class,*" my fourth grade elementary teacher wrote in my report card. It meant little to me at the time, but as I continued through school the label stuck, whether it was in academics, sports, church, or life. Being a leader is an awesome responsibility, and one of the reasons leadership is such a hot topic for me is that I've recognized such a lack thereof. Leadership takes many forms, but always comes back to the basics. One of my friends and mentors, Dr. Sheila Murray Bethel, was the first person I remember who gave me the quote, *"People don't care how much you know until they know how much you care."* When I think of the qualities of leadership I've talked about for so many years, the above quote underlies all of them.

When you look at author, speaker, and leadership expert Peter Drucker's definition of leadership that I've adopted and presented nationally and internationally and then revisit the above quote, you'll see what I mean:

According to Peter Drucker, **Leadership is:**

- *Lifting a person's vision to higher sights.*
- *Raising a person's performance to a higher standard.*
- *Building a personality beyond its normal limitations.*

The rapidly changing environment in which we live makes effective leadership more critical than it has ever been. The future leaders of all organizations who figure out how to encourage their people to change and help them feel good about change are the ones who are going to come out ahead.

Introduction (continued)

One night as my wife and I were lying in bed having our normal chat before turning the light out and falling to sleep, our subject was our adorable blonde haired, blue-eyed niece, Kayla. She had just spent a few weeks at our homes in Myrtle Beach, South Carolina, and Charleston, West Virginia. We missed her!

After the lights went out and my eyes closed, various photographs we had taken of Kayla started running through my mind. Some of the images made me smile and others caused me to verbally say *"Ahhh."* Kayla loves her Aunt Vickie (my wife), and when I recalled the photo of her holding Aunt Vickie's hand and leading her through the woods, it brought a lump to my throat and a scripture verse to my mind. The scripture verse in part says *"...and a little child shall lead them"* (Isaiah 11:6).

As I thought about the fact that leadership always comes back to the basics, I realized that children, too, tend to have a way of bringing us back to the basics. That one photograph caused me to recall others that depicted various qualities of leadership, the same qualities I've talked about for years, but seen now in a basic way, with a child's visual.

I climbed out of bed extremely excited at what had just occurred to me and started sorting through the numerous photographs we had taken of Kayla. The end result culminates in this book, *Lessons on Leadership—Visualizing Qualities of a Leader.*

Kayla Noel Madden lives in Hinesville, Georgia, and was born October 26, 1994. All the proceeds of the sale of this book will be deposited into Kayla's college fund.

Chet and Kayla

> *"...and a little child shall lead them."*
> Isaiah 11:6

Leadership Is...

- Lifting a person's vision to higher sights.

- Raising a person's performance to a higher standard.

- Building a personality beyond its normal limitations.

—Peter Drucker

TRUST

TRUST

Leadership is built on a foundation of TRUST. A trust relationship builds better performance and greater morale.

While attending a conference in Chicago, I once received a phone message from the office manager of one of the companies I own to call her right away. This was an extremely unusual request coming from someone who never contacted me while I was gone, especially since she knew I called the office daily.

When I returned the call she said to me, *"I just fired our receptionist."*

My response was, *"Good!"*

"Would you like to know why?" asked the office manager, somewhat startled by my response.

"No," I responded. *"If you felt that was the appropriate action, then I'm confident you've made the right decision. I trust your judgment."*

In this situation two valuable lessons about leadership were apparent:

1) A leader is smart enough to hire the right people for the job and intelligent enough to get out of the way and let them do it.
2) Employees must be able to trust leaders for support in their decision-making.

To TRUST and be trusted is a requirement of effective leadership.

Leaders Are Good...

COMMUNICATORS

COMMUNICATORS

I n fact, good COMMUNICATORS are those whose ears get more exercise than their mouths.

Dean Rusk, former secretary of state, said, *"One of the best ways to persuade others is with your ears."*

One day I was sitting in my office when a friend stopped by to discuss a problem he was having. He explained his situation and after he finished, got up to leave.

"Thanks, you've really helped me," my friend said as he departed.

I sat in my chair and pondered that statement for awhile before making a move, realizing I had barely said anything at all. Later that day my friend called me to say I had been the fourth person he had attempted to talk to but I was the only one who had listened. The opportunity to talk all the way through about what he was dealing with was exactly what he needed. As he talked through it, he was able to formulate his action plan.

A great leader is not someone who has to be heard, but someone who has the innate ability to listen. It's difficult to have your ears and mouth engaged at the same time. After all, how many times have you heard someone say, *"Oh, they talk real good, they just never listen"*?

Effective leaders are good
COMMUNICATORS not because
of what they say but what they hear.

RARELY PROBLEM SOLVERS

RARELY A PROBLEM SOLVER

D on't you love it when you're sitting in your office having a great day with things going really well and someone comes in and says, *"We have a problem."* How do you react?

Most of the time when someone brings a problem to my attention, I find they've already given it some thought, have a solution, and are waiting for the following question, *"How do you think we should solve this problem?"* By asking this question, you are empowering this person not only to share problems but also possible solutions.

Once one of my managers came to me to share a communication problem he was having with an insurance company. He was clearly frustrated. I listened to the details of what had been done to date and then asked, "What do you think should be done?" He quickly requested permission to make an appointment to have a face-to-face meeting with the decision maker of the insurance company and felt that the matter could be resolved in a more timely fashion. Permission granted.

Effective leaders empower people to solve problems, but RARELY becomes the PROBLEM SOLVER. It leads to good team morale when employees can say "we did it."

Leaders Must Be...

TECHNICALLY COMPETENT

TECHNICAL COMPETENCE

It's as the computer said to the business manager: *"I can be upgraded; can you?"* New technological developments are not just for the young. I wasn't surprised recently when, at the age of fifty-five, I wasn't the oldest member of a computer class. It's not only the business environment we exist in today that demands the need for technical competence, but also our everyday shopping and banking lives.

My son-in-law who works for a high tech company recently asked, *"How can I manage, supervise, and lead a department when I'm not sure of exactly what it is they're doing?"* This was in response to being asked to accept a promotion. He had the skills to manage, supervise, and lead but didn't feel comfortable with his knowledge regarding the particular technical aspects of this new department.

Technology is the most rapidly changing aspect of our lives today. Leaders must stay well read and up-to-date with these changes.

Effective leaders must maintain a high level of TECHNICAL COMPETENCE.

Leaders Must Not...

CONDONE INCOMPETENCE

CONDONING INCOMPETENCE

"**U**ncle Chet, *whoever made these candles ought to be fired; they won't stay blowed out!*" stated Kayla as she attempted to blow out the trick candles.

It amazes me still today when I ask the following question in one of my seminars: "*How many of you have marginal employees on your staff?*" I see hands starting to rise before I tell them not to raise them. Then I ask a more important question, "*Why? Why do you have marginal employees on your staff?*"

If you as the leader of a department, organization, or company realize you have marginal employees, I guarantee you the other employees recognize it as well. As a leader, you lose effectiveness and respect when you condone this. It also leads to a decline in morale and individual productivity in the rest of your employees.

Step to the plate and be effective as a leader by NOT CONDONING INCOMPETENCE.

Leaders Must...

TAKE CARE OF THEIR PEOPLE

TAKE CARE OF PEOPLE

"Mr. Marshall, can you come with me a moment?" an employee once asked. I got up from my desk and followed her to the back stairs, where she showed me a stair tread that was loose and frayed. She was concerned one of the employees would catch a heel and fall.

Some three hours later I was coming out of the men's room and overheard this same employee telling another employee, *"He's already fixed it. He really cares about us."*

As I mentioned in the introduction, Dr. Sheila Murray Bethel, author, speaker, and my mentor, was the first person I heard say, *"People don't care how much you know until they know how much you care."*

Praise is also very important in taking care of people. In one of my seminars I state, *"People work for love and money. Which do you have the most of? Are you willing to spend a little love?"*

Leaders should get up in the morning thanking people, at noon thank more people, and before they leave at night thank even more people.

Effective leadership involves TAKING CARE OF PEOPLE in many ways.

VISIONARIES

VISIONARY

L eaders must have a vision and effectively share their vision.

Leland Kaiser Ph.D., healthcare futurist, is one of the most effective visionaries I've ever come in contact with. In 1982 he delivered a speech entitled "Take Charge of Your Destiny" and shared a vision of a new healthcare industry. He articulated his vision clearly, forcefully, and I will add accurately. During the last several years, I've watched the healthcare industry follow the very outline he shared with us that day. He told us about the good and bad of the managed care arena before it actually happened. I purchased a video-tape of his presentation and use it in my planning retreats to demonstrate the accuracy of a true visionary leader.

The visionary leader takes people from where they are to where they have not been. Show me someone without a vision and I'll show you someone who is blinded to opportunities.

Effective leaders are
VISIONARIES and
agents for change.

Leaders Must...

BE ABLE
TO BRIDGE

BE ABLE TO BRIDGE

Bridges help us get from one side to the other. Oftentimes we don't know what's on the other side, and we don't want to find out because it takes us out of our "comfort zone." A leader crosses these bridges with confidence while building confidence for others to come along. A leader demonstrates that the bridge is dependable, efficient, and rewarding as their people approach a new idea, project, or system.

Bridging two people together who are at opposite ends of the spectrum is also a leader's responsibility. I've sat in numerous meetings in which two people, sides, or factions have had differing opinions. When this occurs, leaders educate themselves on both sides of the issue to bring about the proper bridging to ensure success for the organization.

Effective leaders understand the art and the many aspects of BRIDGING.

WEAR MANY HATS

WEAR MANY HATS

One of my favorite doctor associates had a habit of coming into my office, plopping down in a chair across from me, and declaring which hat he wanted me to put on. He would say, *"Chet, I need you to put on your finance hat and tell me we can afford an additional doctor."* This individual and I were involved in several businesses together as well as being friends; sometimes he wanted only my *"friend"* hat.

Because of our responsibilities as leaders, each question we're asked requires us to put on a different hat. Sometimes it's the hat of boss, personnel director, psychologist, mentor, finance director, operations manager, planner, or just friend. We wear some hats better than others because they just plain fit better, but we've got to be flexible and ready to adjust the fit.

Effective leaders WEAR MANY HATS and wear them well.

Leaders Must Be...

CHEERLEADERS

CHEERLEADERS

Self-worth and self-esteem are healthy aspects of a person's existence. Leaders are not only a part of the team, they are constantly cheering the team on.

The sports figures I enjoy the most are not necessarily the superstars but those who are always in the game, even when they're on the sidelines. They're the ones who even in defeat can find something positive to say. They continue to cheer the other members on, compliment them, praise their performance, and encourage them to keep on going.

In our current environment, money has proven not to be a consistent motivator, but praise and compliments are ingredients that continually work.

Effective leaders are
CHEERLEADERS,
not just part of the team.

VISIBLE AND APPROACHABLE

VISIBLE AND APPROACHABLE

J ust as leaders need to have vision, they must be VISIBLE AND APPROACHABLE.

It's difficult to follow someone you never see or communicate with. Morale and productivity are always raised to a higher level when the leader is available and easy to talk to.

We've all seen people in important positions who try to lead by intimidation, strut instead of walk, inhale but never exhale, frown instead of smile, and love every minute of it. This isn't nearly as effective as leaders who demonstrate warmth and interest in their employees' lives and responsibilities.

In the mid-nineties I decided to semi-retire from one of the organizations I owned to pursue a real passion in life, professional speaking. I was also maintaining two homes in two different cities and simply wasn't at the office as much as I had been in the past. When I was there, I made it a point to go to every person in our company and touch their lives in some way, sometimes by asking questions, sometimes by making statements or telling a story. I always made time for them and demonstrated they were a priority in my life and business.

Do you manage human doings or lead human beings?

Effective leaders must be VISIBLE AND APPROACHABLE so they make other people feel special with personal attention.

Leaders Must...

WALK A MILE IN THE MOCCASINS OF OTHERS

WALK A MILE IN THE MOCCASINS OF OTHERS

I f you have been there, done that, it certainly is a benefit to leadership.

Effective leaders don't work from the sixty-third floor down but from the ground floor up. Titles, position, or income don't make you a leader.

In 1977 I was comptroller/treasurer of a public school system when a new superintendent of schools was named. He was a high school principal being promoted to the superintendency.

When he met with me for the first time, I was impressed. Here was a proven leader who was not afraid to say, *"I don't know, but I want to learn."* Over the next few months we spent a lot of hours together as he learned the basics of school finance. He made it clear he wasn't interested in doing my job, but it was he who would be making budgetary recommendations directly to the board. He also wanted to understand the demanding responsibilities of my job so he could provide adequate support. My department was just one of many he explored to be more effective. He was able to communicate, "I know, I understand and I care." He walked in my moccasins and it made him a more effective leader throughout the school system.

WALKING A MILE IN THE MOCCASINS of the people you're trying to lead is an effective leadership exercise.

Leaders Must...

HAVE A SENSE OF HUMOR

HAVE A SENSE OF HUMOR

There are smoke breaks, coffee breaks, and lunch breaks. My favorite break is a humor break.

Humor breaks are healthy and increase productivity. I love going out in our open work area, gathering everyone around, and telling them an appropriate joke, story, or something funny that has happened to me. Sometimes one of the employees will share something funny with me and I will put them in the limelight and ask them to share their story during a humor break.

It's a proven fact that fun in the workplace makes better employees and improves the environment. Just ask the employees of Southwest Airlines. You never know quite what to expect when you board one of their planes, because their employees have been given permission to have fun in the workplace. Whether it's humorous announcements or harmless pranks played on passengers, when you leave the plane I guarantee you, you've had fun and enjoyed the flight. Southwest Airlines has become number one in employee and passenger satisfaction for a number of years with this philosophy. Try it; you just might like it!

Effective leadership requires a SENSE OF HUMOR.

DECISION MAKERS

DECISION MAKERS

Don't fall victim to what I call the *"ready-aim-aim-aim-aim-aim-aim-syndrome."* You must be willing to fire.

It has been said, *"A decision is what is made when you can't find anybody to serve on a committee."* People rely on leaders to make decisions; leaders empower people to make decisions and then stand by their decisions.

I've learned through the years that every decision makes some people happy and some people not so happy, but that's a part of leadership. Holiday time off always seems to be one of those times when you just can't please everybody. Depending on what day of the week the holiday falls, a decision has to be made with regard to the additional day to be taken. The decision to give the day before or after the holiday as an extra holiday becomes monumental. I normally go with the majority, but those in the minority still complain.

However, effective leaders educate themselves on the issues so they make INTELLIGENT DECISIONS and are satisfied with the results.

INTROSPECTIVE

INTROSPECTIVE

Too many times we look in the mirror and really don't see ourselves at all. Or we do see ourselves and don't take any action to improve or correct what we see. **SWOT** is an evaluation tool I've used for several years not only with organizations but also with individuals.

Strengths, Weaknesses, Opportunities, Threats is what the acronym stands for, and being able to identify these in our individual lives helps us to be introspective. Once we've identified our personal **SWOT**, we can determine the action steps needed to maintain our strengths, strengthen our weaknesses, seize opportunities, and thwart threats, and then set a date for completion. When we do this, we then have a personal plan for the snapshot we've just taken.

Effective leaders are not only INTROSPECTIVE; they are also capable of doing something about what they see.

RELIABLE

BE RELIABLE

In 1972 I assumed a new position as director of finance with a county school system. The department consisted of three employees, all of them with a lot of tenure. One employee in particular had been there for over twenty years and had worked with the superintendent when the entire central office staff consisted of two people, her and the superintendent.

Within a six-month period of time she had tested my diplomacy as well as my Christianity with a lot of challenges. There was one issue in particular that she was very emphatic about and stated, *"I'm not doing it; you will."* I very diplomatically reminded her of her areas of responsibility and that this one fell in her area and she would be responsible. Her response was, *"Well, I'll just talk to the superintendent."* My response was, *"I believe that's a good idea; let's do it now."*

Much to her surprise, when we walked into the superintendent's office, I simply informed him she had something she wanted to talk to him about. As she stumbled over her words and started to explain the issue, he realized the direction she was going and stopped her in mid-explanation.

He said, *"You and I go a long way back. You've been an exemplary employee, but you need to understand one thing right now. You work for Mr. Marshall and he knows what your responsibilities are. If you don't feel you can handle that, maybe you need to find something else to do."*

The superintendent, being the leader he was, gave me confidence that I could rely on him and his support. At the same time, he demonstrated he trusted me to lead and handle the responsibility of the department. The employee was exemplary, and we went on to have a great relationship.

Effective leaders are RELIABLE; you know you can count on them.

Leaders Must...

EXUDE INTEGRITY

EXUDE INTEGRITY

For leaders and followers, *"There is no pillow so soft as a clear conscience."*

Too many people sit in board or committee meetings trying to find a way to do wrong things the right way. It simply can't be done. *"But if we put this procedure code on this procedure, we can get paid for it." "But that's not exactly the procedure being done."* But, but, but… The bottom line is, there is no right way to do a wrong thing.

There was a skit given at our church one Sunday morning for the children that I have never forgotten.

The scene was set in a living room where the father was folding towels from a basket. While doing this task he was reprimanding one of the children who had just lied to the mother about taking a cookie from a fresh batch just out of the oven.

The father was lecturing on the importance of not lying or stealing and how God was not pleased with those actions. He had made his point clear and as the child was walking from the room, the next towel he pulled from the basket had a Holiday Inn logo on it. The father paused when he saw it and the message sunk in.

I heard recently, "Integrity is what you do when no one else is watching." Integrity is a quality without which you can't even think about being a leader.

Effective leaders, practice what they
preach and EXUDE INTEGRITY
(and have no trouble sleeping).

Conclusion

LEADERS CAN'T BE ALL THINGS TO ALL PEOPLE, TRY AS THEY MIGHT.

One of my responsibilities as comptroller/treasurer of a public school system was to present a clear explanation to voters what bond and levy elections meant to the schools financially. I put together what I felt was a very easy to understand presentation regarding the benefits of a victorious election and hit the road to meet the taxpayers.

My first presentation was for a rural high school where 250-300 people had gathered to hear what I had to say. I was well prepared and felt the presentation went well. When I opened it up for questions, three people stood up and took me to task, almost to the point of calling me a liar. Needless to say, I left that night not feeling "Absolutely marvelous" (that is my standard response when someone asks me how I am).

That night I couldn't sleep, as I just continually thought about their verbal attack. At 4:30 in the morning I went to the office. The assistant superintendent for transportation arrived around 5:30. As I walked past his office he greeted me kindly and I just grunted, absorbed in my own personal pity party.

He called me back to his office and ordered me to sit down, saying he couldn't believe how I was acting. He told me he had been present for the meeting and that in the numerous years he had been in the school system he had never heard a clearer explanation or better presentation regarding a very complicated subject. He said, "There were over 250 people present last night and three people got up and took you to task. Those three people would have gotten up regardless of what they heard or who said it." Then he said, "I want to tell you something I want you to remember the rest of your life. The greatest man to ever walk this earth, the greatest leader of all time, couldn't satisfy twelve. How can you expect to satisfy everybody?"

I've never forgotten that very important lesson and as you strive to be the leader you want to be, I trust you'll never forget it either.

Effective leaders do their best and are satisfied with the outcome.

Other books authored and co-authored
by Chet R. Marshall,
available from his Website:

Wholehearted Success
Thriving in the Midst of Change
Magnetic Leadership
Lessons Learned from Bosses On How to be a Boss
My World Peace Can Be Your World Peace

www.elevationexpress.com